The EPIC Series

Text by Michael Brennan
Illustrations and book design by Catarina Neto

www.theepicseries.com

@theepicseriesofficial

For the next generation of Philly sports fans.
Go birds!

The EPIC Game Day

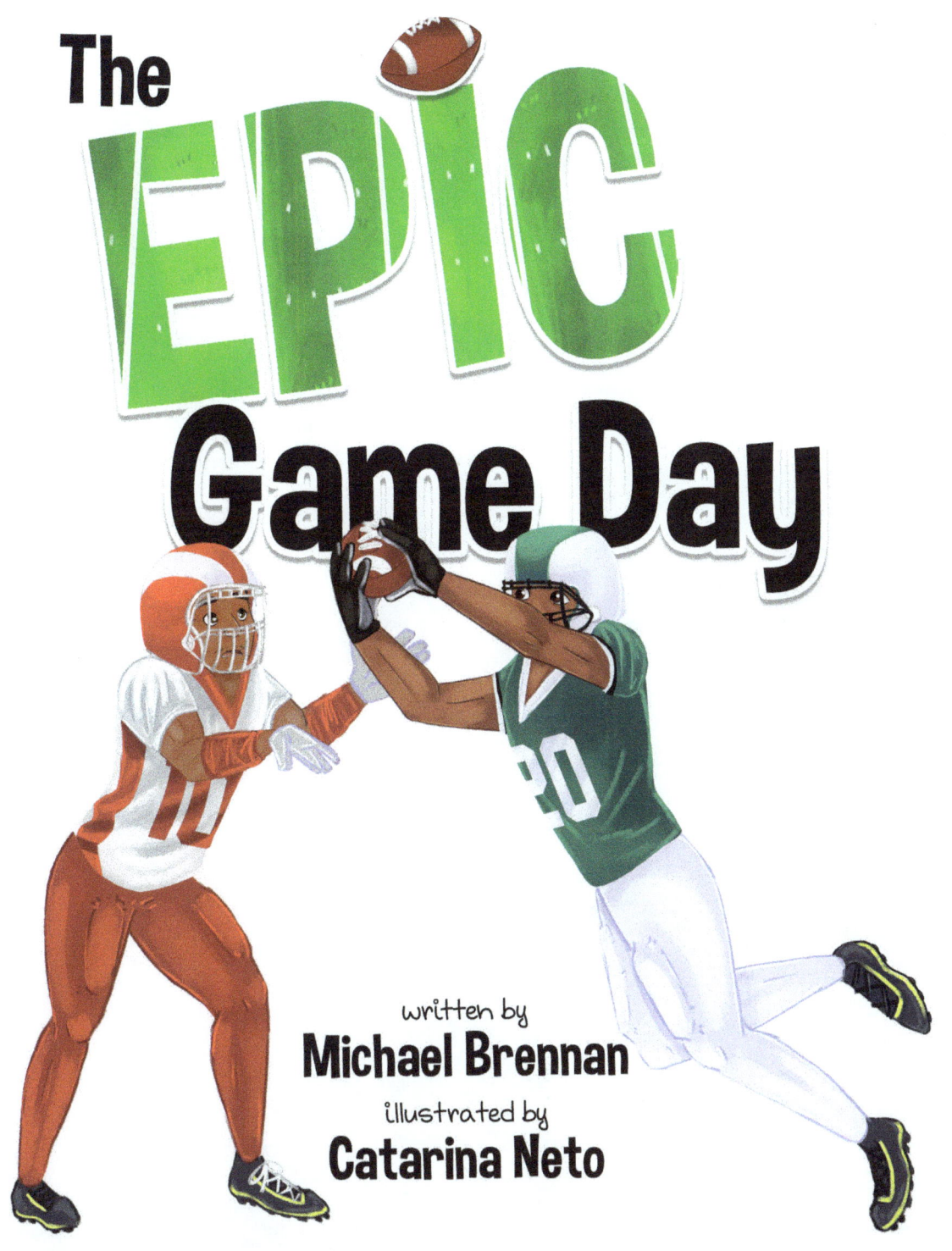

written by
Michael Brennan

illustrated by
Catarina Neto

It's gameday y'all!
Throw on your gear,
Apply some face paint,
And get ready to cheer.

Tailgating's a must,
Let's pack up the grill,
And a cooler with ice,
So the drinks stay chill.

The DJ plays music,
To enhance the mood,
With burgers and dogs,
There's plenty of food.

The pigskin is out,
And cornhole bags fly,
The party is on,
With no rain in the sky.

The weather is perfect,
What a beautiful day.
The teams are warmed up,
And ready to play.

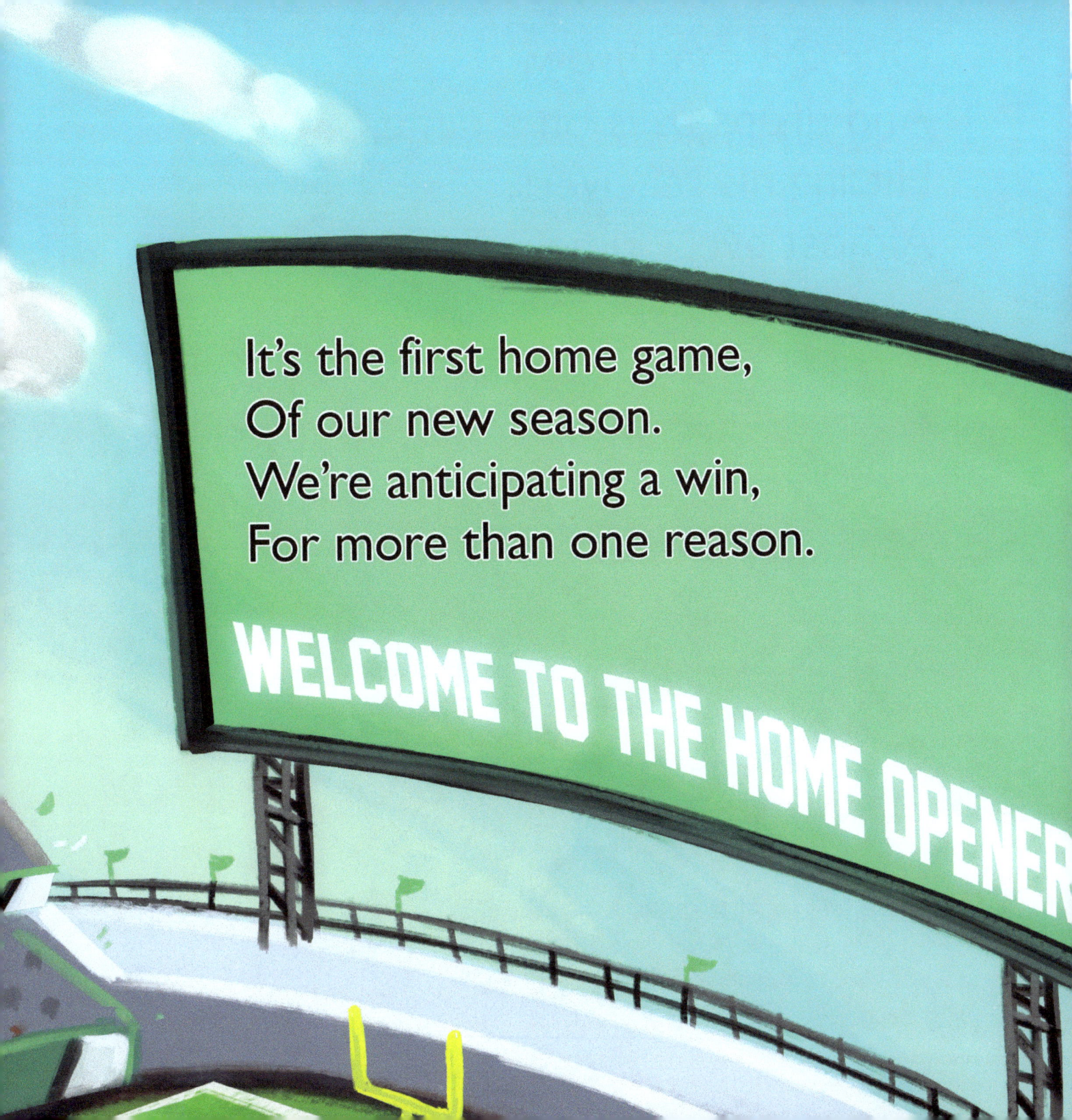

It's the first home game,
Of our new season.
We're anticipating a win,
For more than one reason.

WELCOME TO THE HOME OPENER

Our QB can throw,
And drops balls on a dime,
Hitting his receivers,
Almost every time.

Our running back's tough,
And sprints swiftly downhill,
Shrugging off defenders,
Imposing his will.

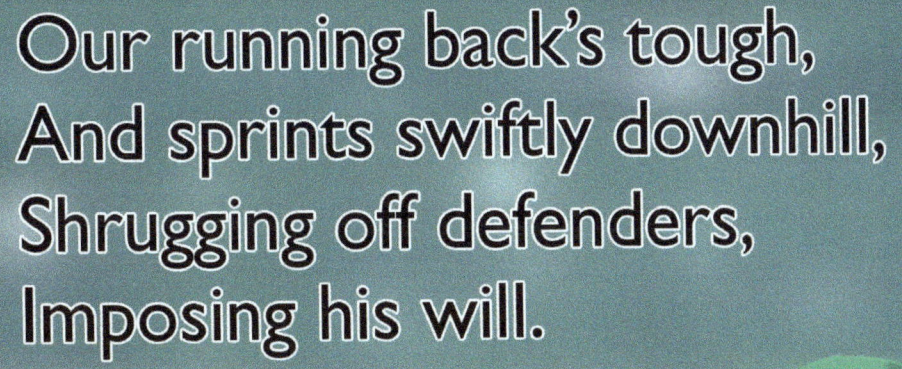

Our wide receiver can catch,
And is as fast as a cheetah.
Challenge him to a race,
I guarantee he will beat ya.

Our O-line can block,
And provide great protection,
Eliminating defenders,
From every direction

Our defense is fierce,
And safeties are quick.
If they choose to pass,
It will be a pick six.

Our D-line can rush,
Pressures their quarterback.
He's got nowhere to go,
And has to take a sack.

Our linebackers are rough,
Always ready to rumble.
If they choose to run,
We will cause a fumble.

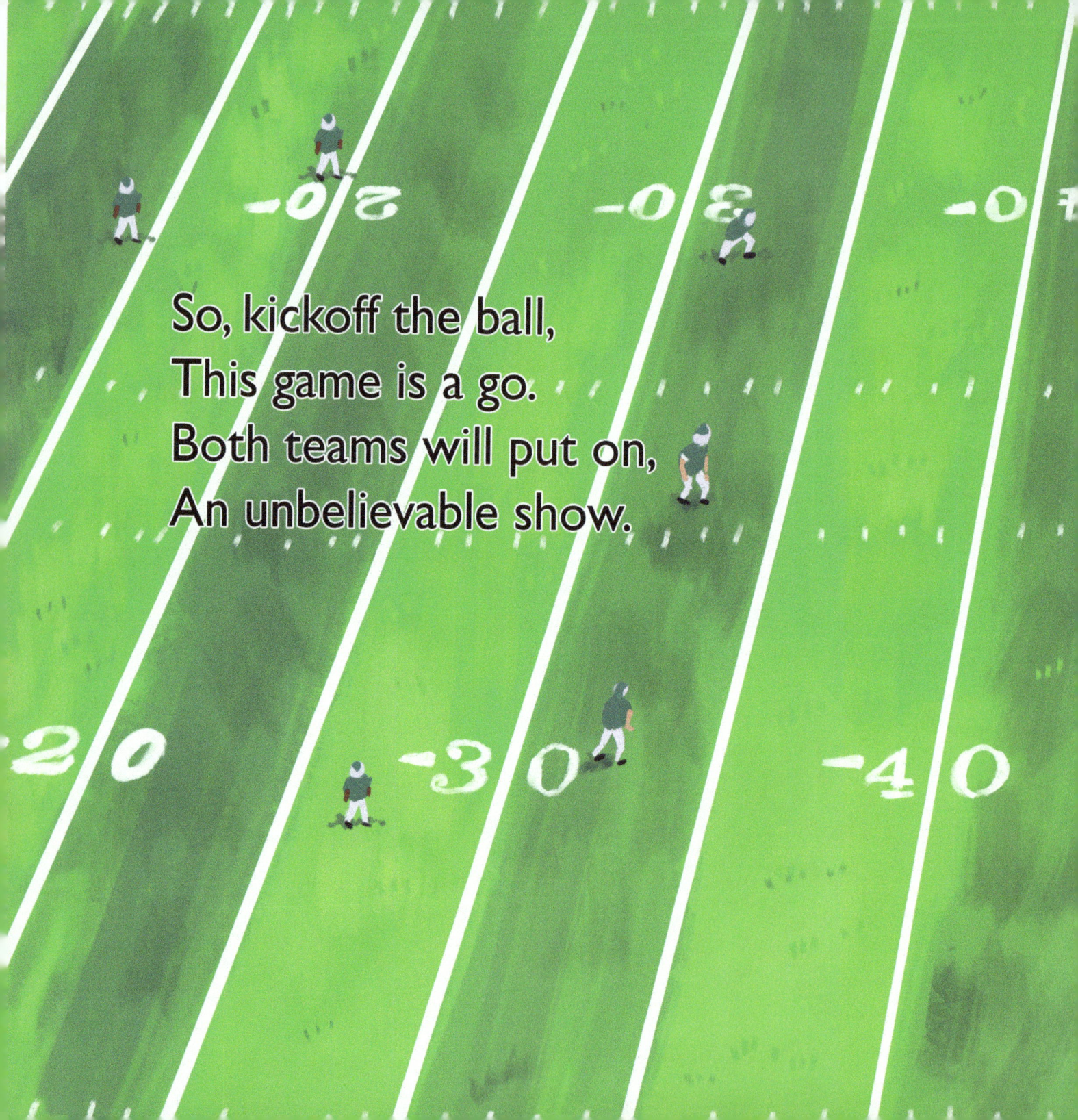

So, kickoff the ball,
This game is a go.
Both teams will put on,
An unbelievable show.

The away team strikes first,
On a short pass.
Our D chased them down,
But ran out of gas.

Then our team drew even,
With a score of their own.
A quarterback sneak,
Into the endzone.

On the ensuing kickoff,
Their returner had speed.
He ran 99 yards,
and put them in the lead.

Our team is behind,
The clock's under a minute,
With one final call,
Do you think they can win it?

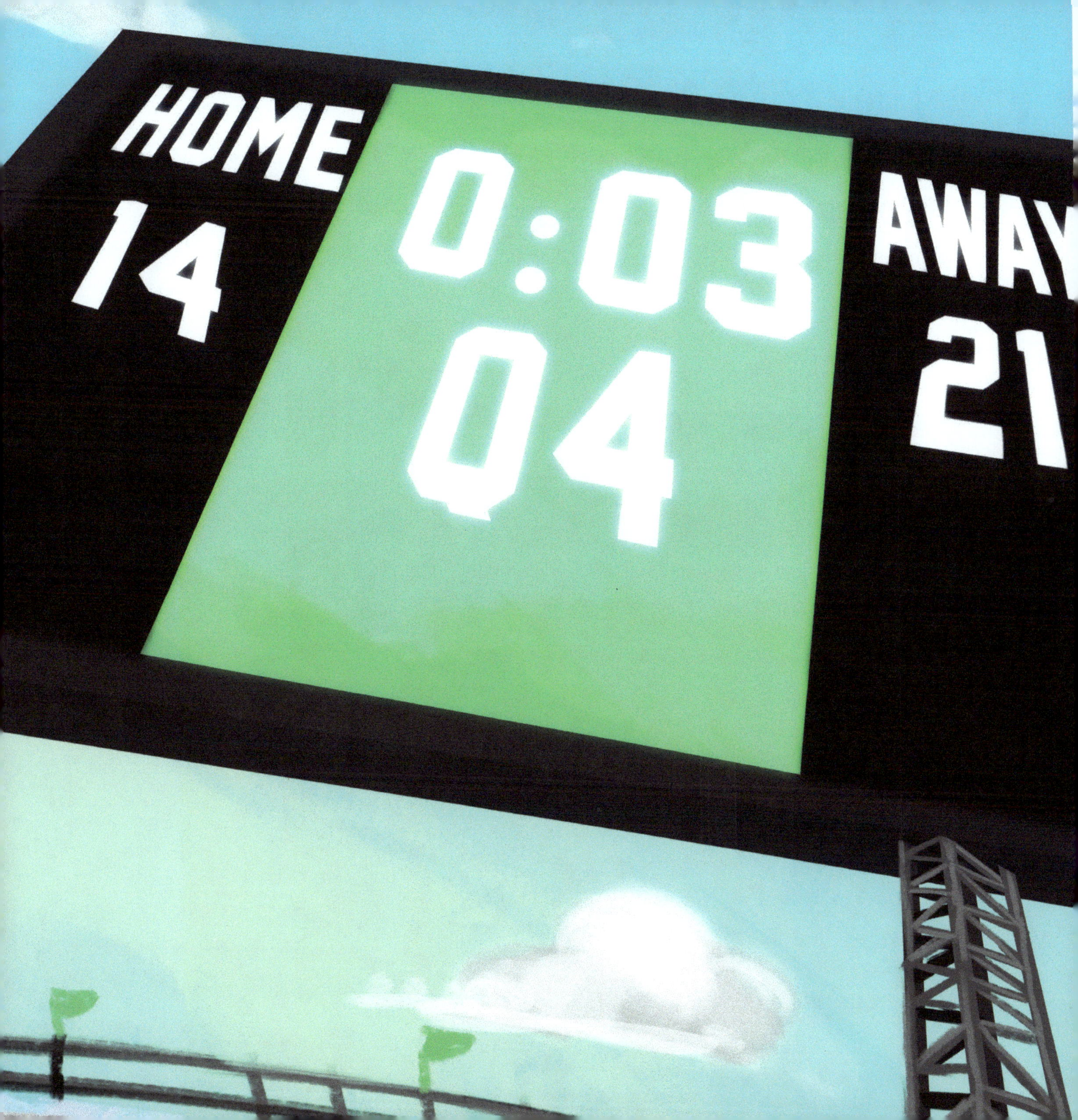
HOME
14
0:03
Q4
AWAY
21

Will they go for the tie,
Or risk it for the win?
They're going for two.
Let's hope he gets in!

The ball snapped in a hurry,
And pitched to the right.
We couldn't believe it,
No defenders in sight!

Crossing the goal line,
With no flags on the play,
A celebratory ending,
To the epic game day!

Overview & About The Author

The Epic Game Day is the third book in "The Epic Series" by Michael Brennan and is a children's book that was inspired by Mike's love of Philly sports. He seeks to highlight the excitement of attending a professional football game and capture the loyalty, dedication, commitment, and love we have for our beloved Philly sports teams. The book portrays the pride we have in our team as well as the ups and downs we endure throughout the game. He hopes this book will inspire the next generation of Philly sports fans with the same passion he had as a young child. Mike currently resides in Bucks County, Pennsylvania, with his beautiful wife, Kimberly, and their son, Brayden. His hobbies include traveling, playing sports, skiing, and enjoying family walks.

Acknowledgments

I wanted to start by thanking my wife, Kim, for believing that I could turn this idea into a finished product as well as supporting me through the entire process. You are the best!

Thanks to my dad who took me to my first Eagles game and continues to be my go-to guy to lock in great seats! I love you!

Thanks to Steve and Sean. My first introduction to football was watching you guys play at Frankford. Steve, you went on to do great things in high school, college, and now currently in the coaching world. Wishing you the best of luck with the Victory Corner Podcast! Sean, your high school games were electric and the college atmosphere was unreal. Some of my favorite memories were watching you dominate under the lights at Camden Catholic. You were both so fun to watch and definitely sparked my love of the game!

Thanks to the 2017-2018 Philadelphia Eagles for delivering the first Super Bowl to the city of Philadelphia. Legend status to the entire team and staff. Also, to the 2024-2025 team for giving us Lombardi #2. The parades were unforgettable!

Thanks again to my illustrator, Catarina. You brought my vision to life and I am forever thankful that I found you. You are a great communicator, pay close attention to detail, and take great pride in your final product. I look forward to working with you on another Epic Series release!